Outward Arrangements

Poems

Francis DiClemente

Also by Francis DiClemente

Dreaming of Lemon Trees: Selected Poems

Sidewalk Stories

In Pursuit of Infinity

Vestiges

Outskirts of Intimacy

Outward Arrangements

Copyright ©2021 Francis DiClemente

All rights reserved.

No part of this book may be used or reproduced in any manner whatsoever without written permission from the author/publisher, except in the case of brief quotations embodied in critical articles or reviews.

ISBN: 978-1-7365403-2-9 (paperback)

Cover art and design by Hamna Jan.

For Pam and Colin

Contents

I.

Crossing Paths	12
Morning Flight Path	14
Aloft	15
Waiting for a Connecting Flight	16
Descent	17
The Last Leaf	19
In Need of Houdini	20
Interment	21
Class Photo	22
Inside the Package	23
Black Trees	24
Squirrel No More	25
Cross on the Side of the Road	27
Scenery on Interstate-81	28
Opening the Memory Book	29
Golden State	30
How to Survive Winter in Syracuse	31
Two Voices	32

II.

No Resistance	34
My Excuse	35
I Hate Poetry	36

Obsession	38
Ithaca	40
Green Screen	42
Coffee Cup Thoughts	43
Imperfect Denouement	45
Born Different	46
Query	47
Entrance	48
The Great Equalizer	49
Parenting Poem (Hanging On)	50
The Equality of Parenthood	52
Nap Time	53
Exam Room Revelation	54

III.

Waiting with Vincent	58
Kiddie Party Planning	60
Church Park	62
Window Watching	64
Vintage Apparatus	66
Pay Phone on the Ground	68
Baby Stroller on the Sidewalk	70
Lonely Tricycle	72
TV Trash	74
Free Shoes	75
Mystery Slippers	76

Finding Chuck	77
Message on a City Block	78
Afternoon in Las Vegas	81
Stars and Stripes	82
White on White	84
The Allure of Trains	85
A Plea for Spring	86
Best Time of the Year	88
The Start of Spring	90
Farewell Summer	92
Snuffleupagus Tree	94
Location Scouting	96
Artistic Path	98
Office Chair at the Curb	100
Sitting in a Pew	102

IV.

Split	106
Warped	107
Beige	108
On the Page	109
Dripping Away	110
Philosophy Apology	112
The Grand Mosaic	113
What You Get	114
An Epiphany	115

Formula for Success	116
Life Label	117
Shift in Thought	118
Resolution of Existence	119
Excel Spreadsheet	120
Multiplicity	121
When Whim Meets Reality	123
Assessment	124
Waiting in a Hotel Room	126
Point of View	128
Road Poem	129
Awareness	130
Game On	132
Fatal Knowledge	133
Thoughts After Sunday Mass	134
Life Enough	135
About the Author	136

I.

Crossing Paths

An old man
passes me
on the street—
shuffling gait,
face twisted
into a scowl,
winter hat
askew on
his head
and a cigarette
dangling from
his mouth.

He goes one way
and I another—
two bodies
sharing the same
oxygen space
with the smell
of tobacco
lingering in
the air.

He moves on
toward his
destination,
unaware that I
will use him
as the subject
of this story—

a poem with no
real ending,
since I don't know
where the
old man went,
or if he made it
safely there.

Morning Flight Path

Three gray-white pigeons
flap their wings
as they dart into
a canopy of trees
outside a nursing home.

Their action reminds
the residents inside
that flight is attainable,
despite fragile bones
and defective hearts.

Yes, the senior citizens
can fly,
at least vicariously,
as long as they can
peer out their grimy windows
and suspend time,
while watching the pigeons
scudding across
the cerulean sky.

Aloft

A line of black birds perched
on a faded red billboard
overlooking Interstate-81
in downtown Syracuse—
feathered sentries
making aerial observations
of life thrumming below.

Waiting for a Connecting Flight

A scrap of trash
that looks like
a flattened paper cup
dances in the wind,
swirling on the tarmac at
O'Hare International Airport.

Set in motion, the debris flits
in accordance with the breeze,
until it rolls away like tumbleweed,
then disappears behind the
tires of a parked truck.

Descent

When turbulence rocks the plane,
rattling the drink cart
and spilling ice cubes in the aisle,
the passengers release a collective gasp.
And as the aluminum tube plummets
in the layers of cumulus clouds,
a little blond girl seated
on her mother's lap
squeals, "Oh, oh, oh."
The woman tries to calm her child,
replying, "Oh is right. Ain't this fun?"

Warm sunlight streams through
the circular windows, bathing my face
as I snap my eyelids shut.
Behind the twin folds
of skin like tan parchment,
my mind rewinds through select memories,
the dots on my timeline
shuttling me to this
point of peril, in this seat, on this plane.

I steady my breathing and begin
reciting a string of Hail Marys,
my lips moving as I appeal
to Our Lady of Perpetual Help
to intervene on our behalf,
to help us get on the ground.
In moments like these, I fear the worst—
an end to my life before I'm ready,
before I've done what I'm supposed to do—
whatever that is.

But I also know we are never ready.
We humans want more time alive,
more days roaming this planet.
And so I keep praying,
asking God to park us safely in Syracuse.
And if it's not to be—
if the plane smashes on impact—
then I ask Him to transport me
to my new home somewhere
beyond these cumulus clouds.

The engines groan, the landing gear drops,
the aircraft descends and
the rolling, tree-lined landscape
of Central New York sharpens into focus.
And today God spares us
relocation to our future residence,
as we touch down on the tarmac—
eliciting applause
from the little girl behind me,
who screams, "Thank you, thank you Mr. Airplane."

The Last Leaf

The last maple leaf
did not want to leave the tree,
even though his mother
told him it was time to go,
time to break free from the limb
and fall to the ground.

The little leaf said,
"Why, why must I leave
when I can still cling to this tree?"

"Because," his mother replied,
"it's part of life, the cycle of nature—
we drop to the ground during fall
and return in the spring.
So come on, let go."

"I will not. I will not," the little leaf said.

But a stiff wind stirred and the leaf
lost his grip and twirled to the earth,
falling into his mother's grasp.

"See, that's not so bad, is it?" his mother said.
"No Mom," the little leaf said.
But then he asked, "Mom, am I still a leaf
if I'm no longer connected to the tree?"

In Need of Houdini

You are wrapped in chains
and stuffed in a metal chest.
The key has been discarded
and the box dumped
into the ocean.

You can't stretch your legs
or flap your arms,
and you're stuck in the box—
unable to lift the latch
and swim free.

How long can you
hold your breath?

Interment

I imagine the coffin lid closing,
the pine box being lowered into the pit,
shovels of dirt hitting the top,
and no one hearing me scream,
"Let me out. Let me out,"
as I realize I've run out of time
to make my life count.

Class Photo

Seeing every person
As a 12-year-old child
Taking a school photo
Eliminates any animosity
You may have for that person.
When you imagine
The awkward kid squinting
At the camera lens—
You discover yourself
Staring back at you.

Inside the Package

When I see
an overweight
cafeteria worker's
butt crack exposed
while he empties
a garbage can,

I think:
the human body
is an ugly receptacle.

But the beauty
it contains,
in the soul it holds,
makes the wrapping
of the flesh so trivial.

Black Trees

The limbs of the black trees
cradle the roadkill porcupine
splattered against the asphalt.
The leaves of the black trees
whisper to the deceased animal,
telling it: "With the spring rain
your bones, blood and quills
will flush into the soil
and fertilize our roots.
Your death sustains our life."
But the porcupine is long gone—
snuffed out by a texter or tweeter
who failed to notice it crossing the street.

And the black trees stand erect
as a storm roils in the distant.
They remain impassive,
aware the forces of nature
could target them next—
uprooting their trunks,
shearing their branches.
And the black trees know
they could soon occupy
the same ground
the dead porcupine rests upon.

Squirrel No More

While walking along Walnut Avenue
near my apartment complex,
I see a dead squirrel splayed
in a shaded area close to the curb—
front paws erect, a rivulet of
brownish-red fluid
leaking from its head.

A fresh kill. A pelt of brown-black fur
pressed against the asphalt
like some animated character
in a *Bugs Bunny* cartoon.

I wonder whether I should call
the New York State Department
of Environmental Conservation.
Does the decaying organic matter
pose a health risk?

Should I pull the squirrel off to the side,
toss it in the high grass
adjacent to the curb?
Or let nature take its course—
with wind, rain and runoff
eroding the animal or
crows eating the meat?

And then more existential
queries fill my head.
Does the squirrel's family miss it?
Are they conducting a neighborhood search?

Will they mourn the loss of their relative?
Do squirrels have souls?
Is there a heaven for rodents?

I don't why this little animal's death
seizes my attention,
but the small figure left out in the open
triggers a sense of pity.

And on this warm, sunny day
with blue skies above me
and trees swaying in the breeze,
with insects buzzing and
flowers bursting with color,
with so much life abounding—
the squirrel gets no more.

No more summers.
No more scurrying across power lines
or cutting through green fields.
No more autumn days
spent climbing trees and storing nuts.

The squirrel's fate
reminds me once again
that death shall come to all of us
in one form or another.
In the end, all mammals will be
spattered in the road.
And I accept this fact
as I continue walking home.

Cross on the Side of the Road

The guy who slid off the highway and died
had no way of knowing he would die
when he woke up in the morning.

He could not foresee his demise
or be prepared for no longer being alive.
He said no special words to his wife
or hugged his kids extra hard.

He simply got up, left the house
and went to work, expecting
to come home in the evening.

He could not predict he would face
the moment we all dread.
And what would it matter if he did?

He had no time to think
about the onset of death.
He was too busy living
to worry about the cessation of life.

Scenery on Interstate-81

Cows grazing in rolling green fields
with heads bent to the ground.
Dense white clouds hovering
in the royal blue sky,
as sunlight filters through
a stretch of trees whizzing by.
Early August in Central New York—
summer fading and autumn advancing.

Yet lake-effect storms and
wind chill conditions remain far off,
as the only thing frozen here
is the memory of this perfect day,
captured and sealed in my mind—
the stored image ready to be retrieved
months from now,
when the doldrums of
mid-February drag me down.

Opening the Memory Book

I love looking at the dates
stamped in old library books.
October 6, 1986.

I backtrack in my mind
to that time and recall
my senior year of high school—
autumn in Rome, New York,
apple cider and piles of leaves,
the roar of the crowd cheering on
the Black Knights football team,
and the crush I had on a girl
that went unrequited.

I see myself walking home alone
on Pine Street with the
stadium announcer's voice
still audible in the distance.

I wonder if that girl
has left the game yet—
if she's locked arm and arm
or holding hands with some other boy.
And would she even know me
if she heard my name?

Golden State

In California, the sun is shining.
In Syracuse, snow is falling.
I want to defrost my toes
by burying them in the sand
at Santa Monica Beach—
watch the waves crashing ashore,
hear the seagulls squawking
and smell the salty air.

But I'm pulled out
of this reverie
by the sound of a
shovel blade
striking pavement
and exhaust fumes
entering my nostrils,
bringing me back to the reality
of a Central New York
scene I can't escape.

I get in the car and
the warm air from the
heater smacks me in the face
as I scan the FM radio stations,
hoping to come across
the Mamas and the Papas
singing "California Dreamin'."
That's as close as I'll get
to the Golden State
on such a winter's day.

How to Survive Winter in Syracuse

The only way to survive
a Syracuse winter
is to think of the snow
as a friend and not a foe.

When you scrape the ice
crusted on your windshield
and the snow clogs the streets,
when your tires spin,
or your car veers off the road—
regarding the snow
as a friend and not a foe
will help you to tolerate the season.

Even when the snow lashes
your face as it blows sideways,
or frozen clumps melt inside your boots,
making your feet cold and damp,
you must remember to
view the snow as a friend instead of a foe.

And what a friend ... a friend that keeps on
giving and giving and giving
six months out of the year.
To which I say:
Thank you, my dear friend,
but I don't need your generosity.

Two Voices

I wanna go home.
Where's home?
Don't know.
You don't know?
Not sure.

OK, so make one here.
Make what?
A home.
Where?
Here.

Can I?
Why not?
Maybe I will.
Good for you.

II.

No Resistance

Poetry invades the
space in my head
and I can't repel it.
The lines of verse
keep coming,
flowing incessantly.

My Excuse

Who cares what I write?
Seriously,
who needs my poetry?

Just what is it
I hope to accomplish
with these jottings,
these inane words
that produce nothing
but silence and rejection?

In my defense,
I confess
I am unable
to resist the urge
to record them.

These things
bubble inside me,
banging away
at my brain
until I relent
and allow them
to spill out on the page.

You see for me
poetry is not a choice.
It's an infection
without an antidote—
a mandate I am
forced to obey.

I Hate Poetry

I hate poetry.
I really do.
I hate how
it gets into
my brain
and won't
let go.

I wish
I could
overcome
my fear
and try
writing
literary fiction
or plotting a
page-turning thriller.

But poetry
just laughs
at me and
transforms
all of my
creative ambitions
into lines
of free verse.

Yes ... I hate poetry,
but it sure
sticks to me.

I guess
I should accept
the best
I can ever be
is a mediocre poet ...
one who hates
writing poetry.

Obsession

A compulsion to create—
a festering desire
to make something from nothing,
forces me out of bed at 5:30 every morning,
planting me in front of my computer,
where I peck away continuously,
typing and typing, stringing together
sentences and passages accruing
into a cohesive idea—or so I hope.

I wish some other hobby
ignited my imagination.
I wish I fancied golf, fly fishing,
hiking in the Adirondacks, craft brewing
or baking the perfect chocolate chip cookie.
I wish my spare time was not spent
writing words that no other eyes may see.

This obsession to lasso the thoughts
assembling in my head
may never amount to anything
more than a few gigabytes worth of files
saved on my hard drive—
Word docs locked in an electronic device—
the computerized version
of the characters in Sarte's *No Exit*.

I realize my work may never
extend beyond this desktop.
But I accept this arrangement,
as I know I can't stop.

Mornings will find me
here in my chair,
coffee cup resting within reach,
and fingers pressed
to the keyboard,
trying to find the right words,
the right notes,
the music and rhythm of language,
and attempting to satisfy
another reader besides myself.

Ithaca

I see a bearded man seated outside
a bagel shop in downtown Ithaca.
He has long, blond hair pulled back into a ponytail,
and he's dressed in shorts and a gray T-shirt.
He's bent over a wrought-iron table,
writing longhand in a spiral notebook,
blue ink filling the page.
Is he composing a poem,
or writing a scene from his unpublished novel?
Or could the words be lyrics for a song
he will sing in a bar tonight?

I am walking with my wife, both of us sipping coffee
while I push our 15-month-old son in a stroller.
The man looks up as we cross the street,
and I realize I am jealous of him,
because I would rather be sitting in his spot—writing.
Does that make me a bad husband and father,
for wanting to abandon my loved ones,
if only for a short time—
to occupy a table at a coffee shop,
to put pen to clean, white paper
and shape words into sentences—
to write something and then possess
the satisfaction of knowing I have written it?

And on the streets of Ithaca,
a Gospel passage comes to me,
a rough translation of Matthew 6:24—
"No one can serve two masters,
for either he will hate the one

and love the other;
or else he will be devoted to one
and despise the other."
Christ's words prove true,
yet I fail to heed His advice,
still laboring to balance
writing with family responsibilities—
never giving either my full time and attention,
and failing them both, equally.

Green Screen

Sometimes I wish I could
"green screen" my life—
alter the circumstances,
change the background,
and transport myself from
my one-bedroom apartment
to a Southern California bungalow.
Employ artifice to shape existence.

But life is a reality show—
just without the scripted confrontations.
And there is no green screen
to fix the disparity between
what I am and what I hope to be.
We either achieve our dreams,
continue striving toward them,
or else give up altogether.
Life provides no special effects
to bend actuality to our liking.

Coffee Cup Thoughts

In what way do you hope
your life will be amended?
What shift do you want to make?
Do you believe in your
ability to change?
And will the world
stand in your way?

Just some questions
scrawled on a pad of paper
while sipping a cup of coffee
in a Panera Bread on a
rainy Wednesday morning.

I guess I'm always
trying in vain to
decipher the enigma
of this life.
But my rumination
brings me no closer
to achieving my goals.

I fail and fail and fail again.
See, now I'm rambling—
as I aim to find
closure to this poem.

But in poetry, like in life,
often there is no clean ending,
no perfect solution,
no tidy conclusion.

Sometimes the words
continue even after
the last line is written.

Imperfect Denouement

Elucidate my misgivings,
cajole my virtue and
sanctify my embrace
are three lines of an unfinished poem
I've carried around in my head
for more than a dozen years,
trying to make sense of the phrases,
decode their meaning and
arrange them into a workable verse.

But I remain stuck, grounded,
unsure of what direction to go.
So the three orphan lines
sit idle and detached on the page—
waiting for companions,
and lingering as ink dried into a
patch of unfulfilled promise.

I can force myself to persist,
to keep going,
struggling to find the key—
drafting the next lines
to knit together an ending.

But what's the point
when the accretion of words
effects no improvement?
When should I decide
to give up writing this poem,
resigning myself to a
failed resolution?
I suppose the time is now.

Born Different

I never chose
to be an artist.

That part of me
came with
ten fingers
and ten toes.

The only
question was:
would I be
any good?

And I'm still
waiting for
an answer,
as the issue
remains unresolved.

Query

I don't have
the answers,
but the questions
keep coming.

So what's the use
of all this asking?

I guess life's
unanswered riddle
makes the living
of it worthwhile.

Entrance

As blood, urine and feces stain the hospital sheets,
a nurse tells a mother-to-be,
"Honey, don't be embarrassed.
What happens in the delivery room,
stays in the delivery room."

The mother-to-be moans and sheds tears
as the epidural wears off and the labor reaches its climax
with a medieval torture method known as "Tug of War"—
sheets wrapped around ankles, legs hoisted in the air
and pulled apart as the mother-to-be screams
and squeezes her muscles and makes the final push until ...
a tiny male human, slimy and alien-looking,
pops out of the womb with a full head of downy, brown hair
and soft, pliable ears like a Teddy bear.

The mother blurts out three words:
"Baby, baby, baby."
The doctor transfers the squirming newborn to her breast,
and the two bond with skin-to-skin contact.
Love and happiness flow.
The task is completed, the effort done.
The child has safely entered the world.
But the real hard work has just begun.

The Great Equalizer

The democratic nature of parenthood.
It doesn't matter who you are—
man, woman or trans, gay or straight,
Black, white or any other shade,
tall or short, skinny or fat, rich or poor—
when your toddler is wailing
in a grocery store or shopping mall,
when the feet are stomping, the arms swinging,
the cheeks reddened and the tears rolling—
all you want to do is pick up the child
and make the crying stop.

Wealth, social standing and comely looks
mean nothing to kids; they're not impressed
by your credentials and you can't negotiate
with these little angels and tyrants who rule the world.
Two clichés apply here:
parenting *wipes the slate clean*
and *levels the playing field*.

All mothers and fathers desire the same thing—
the health, safety and
development of their offspring.
The goals are simple amid the frenzy
of a life marked by stress and lack of sleep.
They are: eat the chicken nuggets, drink the apple juice,
recite the alphabet, put away the toys, finish the milk,
wave bye-bye and go down easy at nap time.

Parenting Poem (Hanging On)

Parenting is an exhausting endeavor
comprised of tugging and pulling,
whimpers and tears,
and a never-ending list of chores:
pouring milk, cooking meals
washing dishes and
doing loads of laundry—
not to mention money
spent and spent and spent
on the necessities your child needs.

Rearing kids saps your energy
and minimizes your finances.
There's never enough time and
you surrender your life
in the service of your offspring.

Some days you feel like saying—
but never dare to speak the words aloud:
Why did I do this to myself?
The thought is horrible
but you can't help it percolating
in the gray space of your brain.
Some days you think,
Why did I trade in my former life?
Why did I give up my adult freedom
for this prison sentence of responsibility?

And then that little child of yours
smiles or laughs, looks you in the eyes,
or wraps his or her arms around your knees.

And then you say, OK, now I know why,
now my purpose for being alive is affirmed,
and you have a reason to go on
despite your weariness.

The Equality of Parenthood

The role of parents:

Holding hands
while crossing the street,
working second jobs,
feeding little mouths,
paying bills and
buying new shoes
and clothes—
all toward the goal
of shepherding them
from toddler to teen
to young adult and
out of the house—
with laughter and tears
along the way.

All parents
are the same.
There's no distinction
among moms and dads
when it comes
to raising children.
We just want
the best for our kids
and hope we can
measure up—
that our best
will be good enough
when tasked with the
hardest job in life.

Nap Time

Late afternoon,
Sunday, gray light
seeping in through parted curtains.

Mother and baby sleeping on the couch,
hair tousled, right cheek against left breast,
elbows curved at equal angles.

I am awake, drinking coffee,
watching their chests rise and fall,
and trying not to make any noise.

My whole life revealed in the space
of three sofa cushions occupied by
two human beings who need me.

Soon the boy will stir;
soon he will squirm and cry, scatter his toys
and race around the cluttered living room.
Soon we will fix dinner
and wash dishes and take out the garbage.

But now time is suspended like a Rod Serling
freeze frame in a *Twilight Zone* episode—
a halting of activity, a pause in my Sunday
leading to reflection and gratitude for my blessings.

Warmth, safety and responsibility
are the words that pop into my head
while I observe mother and child stretched out together.
I don't think about what I lack
or what I hope to attain and achieve.
In this moment, I have everything I need.

Exam Room Revelation

"Autism Spectrum Disorder."
The moment those words
escape the doctor's lips,
our son's future
appears bleaker.
The phrases
"special needs,
delayed communication
and lack of
social interaction" follow.

Sorrow for my son Colin
gushes inside me.
I feel sadness
for the challenges
he will endure,
and for his inability
to have a normal life.

In this case,
love proves impotent.
You can't intercede
with your heart.
And compassion won't fix
the little boy
sleeping in his bed
as I type out
this bad poem
while lamenting
the diagnosis.

But love for him
does not decrease.
Instead, it grows stronger.
I am grateful
for the blessing
of the boy he is ...
and the man
I hope
he will become—
regardless of autism.

III.

Author's Note: The poems in this section originated as the text in Instagram posts. To see the images and posts, go to https://www.instagram.com/francisdiclemente/.

Waiting with Vincent

A scheduled MRI
of the brain shifts
my thoughts toward
all of the
"what if, worst-case scenarios."
While waiting for my name
to be called,
I see a print of *Irises* (1889)
hanging on a wall.

From far across the room,
without my glasses,
the slanted vertical
green leaves
look like snakes
writhing in the dirt.
But the longer
I stare at the image,
the calmer I feel.
Placid is the word
that comes to mind.

And I'm thankful Vincent
spends a few
moments with me
prior to my appointment
with the tube machine.

Because when sitting
in a hospital
waiting room,

artwork by Vincent
never fails to lift the spirits.
A van Gogh painting beats
People magazine
or an iPhone screen
every time.

Kiddie Party Planning

I spot a scrap of legal pad paper
on the ground in the parking lot
of a medical complex in Liverpool, New York.

When I pick it up, I read a list of items
needed for a kids' party.
Some of things jotted down include:
hot dogs, water, sunscreen, juice box,
ice cooler and plastic spoons and forks.
There is also a reference to
yard games, e.g. potato sack races.

On the flip side of the paper
are the following notes:
"Order sheet pizza, order cupcake cake.
Emoji. Approx. 15 kids. Adults?"

I love stumbling upon these little notes
because I feel like I get a glimpse
into the person making up the list,
a snapshot of their thinking process.

I also know that if I were
planning a party for more than a dozen kids,
I would do the same thing—
compose a detailed "To Do" list.

I am curious, however, about the absence
of an inflatable bounce house on the sheet of paper.
And I hope the kids won't be disappointed
when they show up for the party.

- hotdogs
- water
- soda
- juice box
- ice cooler

- yard games
- potatoe sack races

- spunje
- handles bucket
- tent

- sunscreen
- plastic spoons/forks

Church Park

While walking to work
I pass a little park
located next to
Grace Episcopal Church.
It reminds me of the scenery
from the movie *The Quiet Man*.

And in the early morning stillness,
I half expect
John Wayne and Maureen O'Hara
to come striding toward me
along the path.

It's yet another example
of how I have to live vicariously
through cinema,
since I am confident
my feet will never touch
Irish soil.

Window Watching

The stone outline
of a window at
Grace Episcopal Church
reminds me of the words
of Thomas Wolfe from
Look Homeward Angel:
"Remembering speechlessly
we seek the great forgotten language,
the lost lane-end into heaven,
a stone, a leaf, an unfound door."

I consider the meaning
of Wolfe's words
as I stand at the curb,
staring at the facade
of the church,
and trying to imagine
what the window looks like
on the other side of the glass.

Vintage Apparatus

I see a black metal
Underwood typewriter
in a Salvation Army store.
No apps, software updates
or charging required.
The keys feel good
underneath my fingertips.

Pay Phone on the Ground

A metal pay phone
splayed on the ground
near my apartment
building dumpster,
a relic from the
pre-digital age—
anthropological
evidence of
20th-century
American life.
Model discontinued
and no iOS update
to install.

Baby Stroller on the Sidewalk

A stroller parked
On the sidewalk.

No parent present.
No wailing heard.

Just a question
Without an answer:
Where did the baby go?

Lonely Tricycle

A tricycle
left near
a dumpster,
discarded.
Now in need
of little feet
to power
the machine,
spurring movement
on the sidewalk
and evoking
hollers of joy,
while parents
follow close behind.
Or at least
that's what I see
in my mind.

TV Trash

A standard definition television set
abandoned near a tree,
a few feet from the sidewalk.
How many episodes of
The Simpsons did this TV see?

Free Shoes

Brown shoes placed
near my apartment
building dumpster,
looking forlorn,
waiting to be filled
by a pair of feet.
Will they fit me?

Mystery Slippers

Sunday morning:
a pair of white slippers
left near a park bench
in downtown Syracuse.

Questions abound:
Who owns the shoes
and where did the person
sleep last night?

No answers to be found,
so instead cue Johnny Cash's
big, beautiful voice singing
"Sunday Mornin' Comin' Down."

Finding Chuck

The discovery of a pair of Chuck Taylors
underneath a city park bench
leads to a series of questions:

Is the owner walking barefoot at this moment?
Will they return to retrieve the sneakers?
Or were the shoes left behind for another person?

Message on a City Block

A note written on a flyer
posted outside a Dunkin' Donuts store.

The words read:
"What About the Homeless In CNY??
Does Any One Care??"

The message provokes empathy
and a swelling of guilt,
since my answers to the questions
lack sufficient compassion.

Do I care? Yes I do.
Enough to do something about it?
Well, apparently not.

Afternoon in Las Vegas

While I sip
a cup of coffee
outside the
Gold Coast Casino
in Las Vegas,
a stiff breeze
rustles the fronds
of a palm tree
swaying above me,
and shadows hit the
beige stucco wall.

Wind, warm sunshine
and the clear blue sky—
a bit of nature unfolding
amid the tourist attractions—
a respite from the noise
and flashing lights
of the slot machines
on the casino floor.

Stars and Stripes

A battered
American flag
hanging on a
light pole—
the cloth ripped,
the colors faded.

But its glory
remains unblemished
as it flutters
in the breeze—
symbolism
triumphing over
the degraded
condition.

White on White
(Prior to Dome Renovation)

Cumulus clouds
hovering above
the roof of the
Carrier Dome—
the white clouds
like a comforter
covering the
fluffy pillow top
of the Loud House.

The Allure of Trains

A CSX freight train
rushing past me
in East Syracuse.

I step out of my car
and watch it rumble by—
wishing I could

Hop aboard
and become a
westbound hobo.

A Plea for Spring

Dear Mother Nature:
I have one small
Request as the
Calendar turns
From March to April.
Can you give us
More Easter and
Less Christmas,
Please?

Best Time of the Year

Snow finally
giving way
to grass
in Syracuse.

Cold mornings,
but temps
climbing
above 40.

March Madness,
Lenten fish fries
and the crack
of the bat.

Yippee ...
it looks like
we've survived
another winter.

But never forget—
in Syracuse
a lake-effect blast
can still chase away
the Easter Bunny
and send the Moms
scurrying to their closets
to retrieve sweaters
on Mother's Day.

The Start of Spring

Trees blooming
in van Gogh yellow.
I hear buzzing,
see small wings
vibrating in
the branches,
and I know
that EpiPen
season is here.
Time to refill
my prescription.

Farewell Summer
(With Apologies to Ray Bradbury)

The death of summer—
sadness reigns
as the season wanes.

No more soft-serve
ice cream cones,
lakeside walks,
baseball games and
backyard cookouts.

Late August
blues ensue,
giving way to the
birth of autumn.
And you know
what comes next.

Mother Nature
pulls Old Man Winter
down from the attic,
sharpens his dentures
and deprives him of food—
then sets him loose
on the world again.

Snuffleupagus Tree

A fallen tree in Chittenango, New York,
reminds me of Mr. Snuffleupagus
from *Sesame Street*.

And I wonder:
Is my psychological
interpretation accurate?

Did I pass this Rorschach test
inspired by a tree?

Location Scouting

I see a white stucco house with three levels
sitting on a block of East Genesee Street
in my Syracuse neighborhood.

The architecture seems out of place for upstate New York,
so I transport the structure in my mind to a
sunbaked, Southern California setting.

And in the LA film noir projected in my head,
I imagine Lauren Bacall or Barbara Stanwyck
appearing in the top floor window,
dressed in a negligee and smoking a cigarette.

The femme fatale draws back the curtains,
waves to me and invites me in for a drink.
Now I want to push past the establishing shot,
swing the camera inside the house
and write the rest of the plot.

Artistic Path

Strolling through
a walkway with
overhanging trees
near the
Everson Museum
makes me feel
like I have
stepped into a
van Gogh painting.

Office Chair at the Curb

An office chair
transplanted
to the curb.
I hope the worker
who occupied
the seat
was not
terminated.

Sitting in a Pew

An empty church
instills a feeling of peace,
and a sense of being
part of something
larger than yourself.
It's a reminder that for me,
life without faith in God
is meaningless.

IV.

Split

Do you ever get
a sense when you
look in a mirror
that the person
staring back at you
is not you?

There is a separation
between your inner voice
and your reflection
in the glass.

The body and the spirit
do not match,
and the disparity
induces anxiety.

I gaze at my figure
in the mirror and
the sense of self
gets lost—blown away
like cosmic dust—

as I observe
the human matter
shaped into my form,
the baggage of flesh
surrounding me.

And then a
realization sets in:
This must be who I am.

Warped

Who am I?
No really, who am I?
Identity can be transitory,
and a discrepancy exists
between my knowledge of self
and the image I project—

a dissonance between
my aspect and the
voice I hear in my head.
The picture and sound
seem to run out of sync,

and I wonder:
Is this the *me* I think *I am*?
And do others see the same thing
or a different man?

Beige

Beige—the shade of my life,
muted and lackluster.

I want to set myself on fire,
bursting into flaming color—
taking on the pigments of
azure skies,
verdant green fields
and lavender tipped
with morning dew.

But I remain
trapped in the amber
of my bland landscape.
Yet maybe understated
is not so bad—
since beige seems to blend
with everything.

On the Page

Sweep the pink rubber eraser
across the pages of my life—
remove the markings
of my existence—

smear the particles of ink
into incoherent words,
and let the faint lines
end with a period.

Dripping Away

Crack open my skull and
let the cerebral spinal fluid
drip away, escaping like
egg white from a shell.
Then take a sledgehammer
to the cauliflower ball
squeezed inside my cranium.

Now all memories
are washed clean.
No more thoughts, words,
images, fears,
dreams and desires.

Nothing to worry about
since nothing exists—
my life history
drained in the sink
with the soap bubbles
and coffee grounds.

Who am I?
I almost forgot.
Did I forget?
Am I capable of forgetting
if my mind is gone?

Still my heart
goes on thumping,
keeping my life rhythm intact.

Scarecrow departed
but Tin Man still here.

Am I alive
if I don't
realize it,
or really care?
Not a bad feeling.
Nothing to worry about here.

Philosophy Apology

I expect things to be bad,
and when they turn out OK
I'm pleasantly surprised.
I guess I'm a realist
with a pessimistic disposition.

Embrace the futility
is the mantra
I bark to myself.
But this negative approach
spares me from the
disappointment unavoidable
in this life.

The Grand Mosaic

Moments—tiny bits of life
segmented into seconds,
minutes, hours, days.

What matters most is
this time, this place—
dropping your daughter
off at school,
squeezing your
mother's hand,
laughing with
your golf buddies,
feeling the sun
warming your face.

These brief intervals
constitute our lives.
And so I try to exclude
day before and
day after thinking,
because life
is a singular noun
that works best
in the present tense.

What You Get

There is nothing you can do
to avoid becoming dust.
You can try to elongate your life,
but you will expire one day.

And whether cremated
or buried in the earth,
your body will not
survive this world.
Maybe your soul will
travel somewhere else,
but really, who knows for sure?

In this existence,
you are granted only two things:
Right Here. Right Now.
That's all you get.
So make the most of it.

An Epiphany

I've discovered
the key to happiness—
the realization that
there isn't one.

You can't coax
happiness or
make plans for it.

You can only
attain it by accident
through the act
of living itself.

Formula for Success

Life can
be tolerable
when you
relinquish
aspiration
and settle for
acceptable.

Life Label

What's wrong with being average?
Why feel bad if you're not extraordinary?
Don't you know that only certain people
are gifted enough to reach the heights
of wealth, status and glory?

Mediocre is OK.
Decent and hardworking are respectable.
Don't beat yourself up.
Try to enjoy your average,
adequate existence—
as opposed to railing against
a fate you are powerless to sway.

Shift in Thought

At some point
you have to
deal with the
Who You Are
instead of the
Who You Want To Become.

By now the
form is fixed.
You are
complete as is.
Don't expect
anything else.
Don't hope
for anything more.

Resolution of Existence

You must
Live the life
You have
And not
The one
You want.

Excel Spreadsheet

Most adults want a
productive life.
A job. A family. Friends.
A 401(k) and a savings account.
A car. A house. A dog.
A riding lawnmower
And granite countertops.

But there is a difference
Between *WHAT WE WANT*
And *WHAT WE GET*.
We are comprised of the
Choices we make
And the plans we formulate.

Life is both a
Struggle and a blessing.
But it's all we have,
And it's all we're given
Between birth and death.

Time wanes
And the span is short.
So get on with it—
Seek, strive and toil,
But be willing to settle in—
Before you miss the living
And find out it's too late.

Multiplicity

As I've gotten older,
I've come to realize
I am not a single man
but many, wrapped together.

I am a kind man
who loves his neighbor.
I am also a miser
who refuses to add one dollar
to my grocery store total
to support
St. Jude Children's Research Hospital.

I am a practicing Catholic who worships
the Father, the Son and the Holy Spirit.
I am also a sinner who screams
Christ's name in vain
when I stub my toe
or spill coffee grounds
on the kitchen floor.

I am a gentle person who calmly dresses
my four-year-old son, singing to him
as I put on his hat, boots and gloves.
But I am also an impatient man
with an Italian temper
who fulminates over stupid things.

Good and bad.
Benevolent and hostile.
Affable and churlish.

Decent and salacious.
These are the parts that make up me—
several layers of the self
folded into one body, one brain, one personality.

When Whim Meets Reality

My ambition is greater
than my talent.
I realize now
I will never
accomplish my goals.

I rage inside
at the ineffectuality
of wanting so much
but getting so little
out of a life
I cannot control.

I must scale back
my dreams,
accept minor success,
a whisper here,
a trickle there,
while at the same time
renouncing the hope
that condemns me to failure.

Assessment

Success eludes me.
At age 50,
I am not
where I had hoped to be
at this point in time.
My career lags
and money remains scarce.
I rent a one-bedroom apartment
and drive a used Honda CR-V.

Fear, indecision,
poor choices and
circumstances share
the blame for my
current state of mediocrity.

But I chastise myself
for a lack of gratitude,
remembering I have
so much to be thankful for.

A partial list follows:
I am upright.
My heart pulsates,
my blood pumps,
my legs carry me
where I need to go.
And I have a family
who loves me
despite my selfishness.

I see two choices
for my future—
acceptance or
continued dissatisfaction.
I attempt the former
but propense toward the latter.

So I ask:
Can I live with
this version of myself
without condemning
the man I have become?

And can I let go
of the desire to be
more than what I am
right now—
knowing improvement
is unlikely?

Waiting in a Hotel Room

Mid-morning, empty hotel room in Manhattan.
The air-conditioning unit roars to life,
overpowering the street noise,
and the green numbers
on the digital alarm clock read 10:36.

I am waiting for the minutes to count down
before I must leave for a video shoot in Queens.
I sit upright in the desk chair,
resting my back and knees, storing up energy
before my body will be called into action,
lifting camera cases, carrying tripods and light stands
and pushing an equipment cart loaded with video gear.

I am a 50-year-old man with severe osteoporosis
complicated by compression fractures
in the thoracic and lumbar regions.
How much more strain can the brittle spine take
before the vertebrae implode,
before the bones are pulverized into dust?

I reflect on my profession and consider what skills
and experience I possess at this advanced age.
Am I competent enough to secure a different job—
one that requires more intellect and less physical strength?

But this is just a short poem—throwaway words
scribbled in a pocket notebook,
thoughts unspooling while waiting
for the clock to hit 10:45 a.m.—

departure time for our video shoot.
The minutes tick away and my tarrying ends.

Rise, I tell myself.
Switch off the desk lamp
and move across the thin, navy blue carpet.
Open the door and exit the room.
Allow effort to conquer anxiety.
Let motion and activity chase away
these Thursday morning meditations
imbued with self-pity.
Go downstairs and do your best today.

Point of View

Look outward
beyond yourself—
flee the space
inside your head,
and seek the magic
of the world instead.

Road Poem

Follow the ribbon
Of the road.
Let the lane
Of life guide you.
Go forward with
Gas pedal engaged,
And travel safely
Into the unknown.

Awareness

How many people are dying
in emergency rooms
at this exact moment?
Right now, how many people are
exhaling their last breaths?
How many loved ones
arrive too late to say goodbye?

Each day ushers in death—
and while we sleep,
smashed brains, shattered bones,
plugged arteries, faulty hearts,
cancer and other diseases
claim their victims.

We try not to notice.
We try to avoid the truth.
We rush about our lives,
never knowing when
our time will come—
until one day it does.

I can't live like that.
I can't avoid the obvious.
I need to face death daily,
to recognize it lurking, prowling,
ready to pounce on me.
This knowledge of death
creeping nearby forces me
to examine my existence

and ascertain if I am useful—
wise with my time or wasteful.

I accept the finite offering
of a limited lifespan—
what little measure
of time God has granted.
It's up to me to make it count.

Game On

No one wants
to say goodbye,
but life chooses
the day we die.
The rules are rigged,
the fix is in,
but oh
how we love
to play the game.

Fatal Knowledge

You are one cut away
From bleeding to death.

One misstep from a fall
That breaks your neck.

One wrong turn
From a fatal car wreck.

But life should be more
Than the avoidance of death.

So don't let fear of the end
Dictate your path.

Thoughts After Sunday Mass

Do not be afraid.
Death is not the end.
You will go on
After your life is done.
All you can do is
Trust that God will
Activate the next phase.
And if by chance He doesn't—
Don't worry—
You won't know about it anyway.

Life Enough

Are we more than the
thoughts we cogitate,

more than the hopes we have
but do not express,

more than the heights we seek
but fail to reach?

And are we OK
with who we are

when we turn out the lights
and go to sleep?

About the Author

Francis DiClemente is the author of five previous poetry collections, most recently *Dreaming of Lemon Trees: Selected Poems* (Finishing Line Press, 2019). He lives in Syracuse, New York, and his blog can be found at francisdiclemente.com.

www.ingramcontent.com/pod-product-compliance
Lightning Source LLC
Chambersburg PA
CBHW040423100526
44589CB00022B/2814